Gerhard Frank

Creative Soccer Training

Meyer & Meyer Sport

Orginal title:
Fußball–Kreatives Training
- Aachen : Meyer und Meyer, 1998
Translated by Robert McMurray

British Libary Cataloguing in Publication Data
A catalogue for this book is available from the British Libary

Frank, Gerhard:
Creative Soccer Training/Gerhard Frank (Transl. Robert McMurray)
- Oxford: Meyer & Meyer Sport (UK) Ltd., 2001
ISBN 1-84126-015-0

Oxford, Aachen, Olten (CH), Vienna, Québec, Lansing/Michigan, Adelaide, Auckland,
Johannesburg, Budapest

Member of the World
Sport Publishers' Association (WSPA)
www.w-s-p-a.org

Cover Photos: Bongarts Sportfotografie GmbH, Hamburg/Polar Electro GmbH, Büttelborn
Photos: Hans Jürgen Becker, Elkerhausen
Cover design: Birgit Engelen, Stolberg
Cover and type exposure: frw, Reiner Wahlen, Aachen
Editorial: Winfried Vonstein, John Coghlan, Paul Cooper
Printed and bound in Germany
by Druckpunkt Offset GmbH, Bergheim
ISBN 1-84126-015-0
e-mail: verlag@meyer-meyer-sports.com
www.meyer-meyer-sports.com

Creative Soccer Training

Contents

Throughout this book, the pronouns he, she, him, her and so on are interchangeable and intended to be inclusive of both men and women. It is important in sport, as elsewhere, that men and women have equal status and opportunities.

Foreword

Soccer is best learned by **playing**. Playing with the ball teaches a feeling for the ball, timing, individual technique, confident ball handling, accurate goal-kicking, creativity, fun and a sense of humour on the field.

There is nothing worse for a soccer player than training without a ball, which is why the ball must always be the centre of the training session. In soccer the ball creates the greatest motivation for training, not only for young people, but also for older players.

With the ball at his feet the player quickly forgets the strain of a hard physical training session, and renewed enthusiasm increases the will to train and imagination in handling the ball.

Formerly **street soccer** with a tennis ball, tin can or a piece of leather in the shape of a ball was the stimulus in soccer games, with a goal at each end of the street.

Unfortunately no one plays "street soccer" any more. In those days the ball was always the centre of the game. Uncomplicated and played for fun, enjoyment was the most important part of the game. And this is how training should be again today.

The first signs of holistic soccer training can be seen in **"Soccerball"**, **"Calcetto"**. This form of playing came from Italy, where small pitches can be found in the middle of the city, and where the players play **"five against five"** using small goals.

Whole suburbs field a team and compete for the **"Copa Municipale"**, or City Cup. In this way the clubs discover many talented up-and-comers.

The ball is the medium. With it the player learns to develop and improve his own individual technique and to do the right thing in any given situation during a game. Training playfully does not just mean "dribbling, trickery and feinting", but can also contain good, hard physical conditioning and training in tactics and technique.

The "play" method of training suggests itself here automatically.

The advantage of the "play" method of training is that every player can compensate for his strengths and weaknesses by "playing".

With the help of the "play" method every coach can succeed in designing a systematic, varied and exciting training session.

My special thanks go to Meyer & Meyer Publishing, Dr. Irmgard Jaeger of the same company, photographer Hans-Jürgen Becker and, last but not least, my "actors" Alexander Bendel, Alexander Maus and Sascha Vinogradic, who carried out the stretching exercises.

One final note: for technical reasons males and females are referred to in the text in the neutral form.

Gerhard Frank

Introduction

Modern soccer means speed, dynamism and toughness. Technical refinements and showpieces have only scarcity value. Even in the German Bundesliga there are still players who play as if they have two left feet, lack technical perfection and who thus experience constant difficulties in critical situations during the game because they have not learned to use both feet.

We are born with some motor skills, others are also easy to develop and train; this can be done by specialised practice. The ball should be the centre in soccer practice right from the junior years; indeed, no training session should be carried out without it. Mindless training of condition should have no place in modern soccer practice.

Children's fascination for the ball must be used in everyday training. A training session is interesting when the coach makes it realistic.

The aim of soccer training is to bring the performance of each individual team member, as well as the whole team up to as high a level as possible.

The contents of the training session are determined by the players' age, development and performance, as well as the current situation of the whole team. Championship hopes as well as the fear of being relegated to a lower league are also a deciding factor.

The physical demands that characterise a soccer player vary. During a game the players are subject to demands of all sorts, varying from the negligible (walking, jogging, standing) to the maximum (sprinting with and without the ball, stopping, turning, jumping to head the ball, tackling etc.).

All these demands can be imitated and compensated for by realistic training. Physical fitness i.e. strength, endurance, speed, coordination and flexibility may be developed, improved and corrected in precise coordination with each other by means of realistic exercises. Nevertheless the coach should hold speed, strength and endurance training with specific exercises at regular intervals.

Tactical objectives can be practised easily and effectively in game-related exercises. This is an excellent way of teaching and learning team tactics such as zone marking, pressing, forechecking, hand over, take over, moving to the ride of the ball.

An immediate check by the coach enables the players to experience success quickly and creates renewed motivation to try out and apply new tactics.

Through similarly structured coaching, skill at the game and playing behaviour can be developed, trained and practised in a competition oriented atmosphere.

Competition oriented training is an excellent way of learning and improving psychological and mental skills, willpower, courage, decisiveness and stability.

2 Skill and Behaviour on the Soccer Field

In order to develop playing skills and behaviour in a match-oriented training, these must first be clearly defined.

Playing skills may be seen not only as the sum of technical and tactical skills and physical ability, but also as a physical, sport-related requirement, and variety of actions corresponding to the constantly changing circumstances of a soccer game.

The level of playing ability is determined by the quality of the individual players ability to make decisions and to find his orientation on the field. The degree of the player's ability to cooperate enables him to act according to the demands of each situation and imaginatively in a competitive situation.

The ability to anticipate, willingness to accept risks, and ball-skills are also part of well-developed playing skills.

PLAYING SKILLS

1. Anticipation Skills
Recognising and distinguishing complicated movements determined by the initial situation, and its following changes with fellow team members, the ball and opponents. The recognising of game related signals (acoustic, optical and tactile).

2. Decision Making Skills
This is the quick conversion of movement stimuli into motor actions. The recognition of spatial and chronological game actions through specific activity. The quick comparison of past experience with present playing (tactical and motor memory).

3. Playing Speed
The rapid joining of individual movements into whole movements through reaction speed, power speed, and maximum acceleration ability.

4. Moving with the Ball; Creativity with the Ball
The developing of a feeling for the ball, learning to experiment and feint with the ball. The coordination of motor and ball handling skills in a spatial and chronological sequence.

5. Willingness to Take Risk

The development of a sense of responsibilty and readiness to make decisions for risky moves.

6. Team Spirit and the Ability to Work with other Team Members

The development of group tactics and tactical principles as well as the verbal and non-verbal exchange of information between individual team members.

Playing behaviour is reflected not only in the technical perfection of individual moves, but also includes conscious performance behaviour before and during the game.

Depending on the personality of the individual player, playing behaviour manifests itself not only in one's own psychological and mental skills but also in one's own individual behaviour. Physical condition also has a decisive influence on the player's technical and tactical playing.

PLAYING

1. Technical Perfection and Originality

The development of motor skills and surprising, unforeseeable moves. The shaping of individual characteristics in ball handling.

2. Stable Physical Performance

The development of a constant level of general and soccer-related physical fitness. The creation of a high degree of tolerance to stress during training and playing, the ability to counteract distractions. Development of stability in one-on-one situations.

3. Tactical Behaviour

The development of tactical playing through position related behaviour. The development of tactical discipline under pressure. Fulfilling demands made by the position being played, including those against one's own preconceptions and inclinations.

4. Social and Ethical Behaviour on the Soccer Field

The development of fair and socially acceptable playing behaviour with one's own team-mates and opponents, even with personal disadvantages e.g. loss of points or goals. Respecting the decisions of the referee and keeping one's temper when fans and spectators yell abuse.

3 The Necessity of Planning Training Units

Apart from the different methods of planning a training unit, it is necessary to understand the structure of soccer and to convert this into a game-related form of training.

The laws of general and specialised theories of training must also be observed when redesigning training according to the "fun" method, as used to be the case in traditional training planning.

The player must not get the impression that isolated skills training has lost its importance. Rather, just practising techniques can help the young player to practise certain patterns, e.g. ploys and feints, again and again so that they become automatic, such as the "Stanley Matthews Trick", the "Beckenbauer twist" or "the Push".

When planning a unit the experienced coach should keep in mind the predetermined objective and the individual parts of the soccer season. Not every soccer training programme can be used at the same time. The principles of training periodisation apply here too.

Even the principle of "overcompensation" makes demands on "creative training" that are relevant to training.

Seasonal and competition breaks in winter and summer must be taken into account when choosing a particular form of training, so as not to produce one-sided training load or even incorrect load (overtraining/undertraining).

Example: The team has just finished an exhausting game. The next training unit should not contain any form of game that makes demands on the players' anaerobic endurance, because the hard game has used up all the stored carbohydrates which must first be replenished.

4 Symptoms of Strain and Susceptibility to Injury

Recent studies in soccer have shown that the weekly loads among members of the German Bundesliga have increased dramatically, while recovery time is far from sufficient. The number of injuries, especially in the top clubs, has increased drastically.

Wrong amounts of training, both in pre-season activities as well as in the Bundesliga season, seem to be responsible for this. Recovery phases, however, are an important part of the overall training plan.

Blood lactate measurements can measure the players' current ability to cope with load, but by themselves do not convince as the best method of controlling training.

Urea checks are an important contribution to improving the quality of training. Investigations of players in the First Division of the Bundesliga, and in amateur leagues, as described by WIENECKE, demonstrate a close relationship between higher urea levels and increased susceptibility to infections and injuries (c.f. WIENECKE, E. in: "fußballtraining", Vol. 4, 1997; p 29 ff).

The parameters of the investigation clearly showed excessively high load during training sessions and competitions over several weeks. Levels of from 9 to 10 mmol/l indicate excessive load during training. Signs of overtraining may be easily detected through urea checks. The opinions of coaches and players as to what constitutes the right amount of training are no longer sufficient, and lead to the wrong conclusions on the subject.

A appropriately designed recovery programme can make a valuable contribution to training sessions. Active recovery training such as cycling, running, aqua-jogging etc. is preferable to passive measures such as massages and baths. Ideal conditions may be achieved especially by cycling on flat surfaces in low gears.

Aqua-jogging affords relief for joints, muscles and ligaments. Here, joints and muscles are put under gentle strain by the physically buoyancy. The additional massaging effect of the water accelerates the breakdown and removal of fibre (see the chapters on "Warm-up" and "Cool-down").

Even training according to the "play" method does not release the coach from carrying out regular checks of the training loads, and from following these up with the appropriate recovery training.

5 The Advantages of the "Play" Method

There are six arguments in favour of training according to the "play" method:

- Playing with and around the ball boosts everybody's motivation.

- Simultaneous psychological, physical and tactical training - mind and body form a unit or, to put it another way, head and feet are in unison.

- Differentiating according to age, performance level and training state - children have different training emphases, and train with different intensity and different volumes than adults.

- The improvement of harmony and communication within the team - the motto "all for one and one for all" promotes team spirit.

- The promoting of individuality - everybody can be Pélé, Ronaldo or Elber.

- Creativity and imagination make intelligent playing possible - quick reaction to the tactics of the opposing team and one's own actions increase playing efficiency and a shared feeling of success.

6 Does this Method Have Disadvantages?

Many say that soccer players are lazybones in training. My experience has shown this to be the case for only a tiny fraction of players.

Playing forms of course conceal a certain risk, since one player or another may not pay full attention to the required task for a few moments while unobserved. The coach must recognise this failing and change it through individual training, and a personal talk with the player concerned.

A further disadvantage could be in the high effort of the way coaching must be organised, as the coach has to look after several teams with differing demands on work at the same time. After a settling-in period, however, this can be easily overcome.

7 Putting Match Tactics into Game-related Training

How can tactics be taught by "playing"?

First of all a few important questions concerning the general external and internal conditions need to be clarified:

* Which age group is being coached - Juniors, Seniors, Ladies or veterans?

* Which division does the team being coached belong to - county, local, state, association, top, regional, or national league?

* What sorts of players are available at the start of the season - players from lower or higher leagues?

* Which playing concept is preferred - attacking or defensive?

* How have the new players been trained - attack minded or defensively; are they technically competent, aggressive playing types?

* What intellectual interest in tactics can one assume the players to have?

* What new basic tactical concept is to be used - strong defence, counter-attack, playing on the wings, forechecking, pressing?

Only after these questions have been answered the coach can set down the coaching plan and tactics.

The basic external conditions such as the equipping of the playing field, practice equipment (balls, cones, slalom stakes etc.) must be given the appropriate consideration when training according to the "play" method is being planned.

8 Eleven Important Points on Methods and Organisation

1. Warming up training can be carried out in isolated elements such as running, stretching and running, or be more closly related to the main point of emphasis of the training unit. Such training should always include the ball. Small groups - for defence, midfield or attack - can warm up together or separately; this promotes cooperation and team spirit (see the chapter on "Warm-up").

2. The choice of training units should be guided by the content of the last unit and by the last game respectively. The intensity and extent of the training units must take the players' current training condition into consideration.

3. New exercises should be phrased and explained very clearly. A demonstration promotes understanding and clarifies any existing problems. Here as well the tried and true principle "from the unknown to the known; from the easy to the difficult" applies. The coach corrects any mistakes the players may make.

4. The players should be actively involved in the selection and variation of individual exercises; this increases attention and interest in training. Suggestions from the players should be commented upon positively - this increases players' motivation.

5. In choosing the exercises, suggestions and tips can be borrowed from other sports and adapted to suit soccer e.g. a quick change from attack to defence (basketball). After losing possession of the ball every player runs to a previously determined position, thereby covering a defined area or zone.

6. After intensive exertion with high pulse, lactate and urea levels, the players should have an active rest period with stretching and loosening-up exercises (psycho-physical recovery).

7. When putting the exercise groups together, attention should be given to changing partners in all groups - new partners and opponents increase motivation and playing pleasure. A variation in the game content should be made in the different age and performance groups.

8. The selection of the types of games takes place in close coordination with the weekly programme (number of games, number of training sessions).

9. It is a good idea to use the markings on the playing field when dividing up or adding to the various pitches or corners; but only where necessary. In this way additional opportunities are created for varying the ways of making the best use of the whole pitch (see the chapter on "Making the Best Use of the Pitch").

10. At the end of a session a so-called "cool-down" should be carried out: jogging around the field with relaxing and stretching exercises (see the chapter on "Cool-down").

11. If a concluding game 11:11 is played, the coach should demand of the players the tactical, technical and physical elements in the game that they have just practised.

9 The Effects of Altering the Training Game

If a game form is altered this can mean a relief, but also a complication. The alteration in content depends on the objectives those whom this form of training is aimed at (children, teenagers and adults), and the grade and strength of players and team.

Complications
- Limiting the available playing area (reducing the size of the pitch).

- Limiting playing time (having to score goals within a certain time).

- Limiting ball contact (only two or several touches) for everybody, individuals or groups.

- Limiting the size of goals (reducing the size of the goals: 5 m or 3 m wide, normal height or 1.5 m or 0.5 m).

- Limiting the number of players (games are played with more or fewer players or one team is larger than the other).

- Limiting the available resources (one, two or several balls).

Relief
- Increasing the size of the playing area (enlarging the pitch).

- Extending playing time (scoring goals without a time limit).

- Extending ball contact (free play with dribbling, feinting and swerving).

- Altering the number of players (the number of players is increased or reduced).

- Altering the number or size of goals (bigger goals, several smaller goals)

- Different ways of scoring goals (goals may be scored from the front or from behind).

- Varying the counting points for particular goals (goals scored with the head or the "weak" foot count double).

Note: The above list is not exhaustive. Each coach should develop some creativity of his own and think up a few more variations.

10 Making the Best Use of the Pitch

The use of existing markings on the pitch is a top priority.
In addition it can be sub-divided into smaller pitches of varying sizes (see Figures 1-4).
The coach needs marking materials e.g. cones, stakes, flags, marking tape, marking cart with chalk etc. The railings around the field can also be used, coulered painted as goals.

The enlargement or the reduction in size of the playing field, has certain effects on whichever form of game is selected.

Here are the most important features of an enlarged pitch or one reduced in size:

Large field	Small field
• The players have longer distances to run/less ball contacts	shorter distances to run/ more ball contacts
• More time to stop and control the ball/to pass it	Less time to stop and control the ball/to pass it
• The ball has to be passed over longer distances/less dribbles	Shorter passes/more dribbles
• Less tackling	More tackling
• Longer breaks/less pressure	Shorter breaks/more pressure

11 Changing the Size of the Pitch

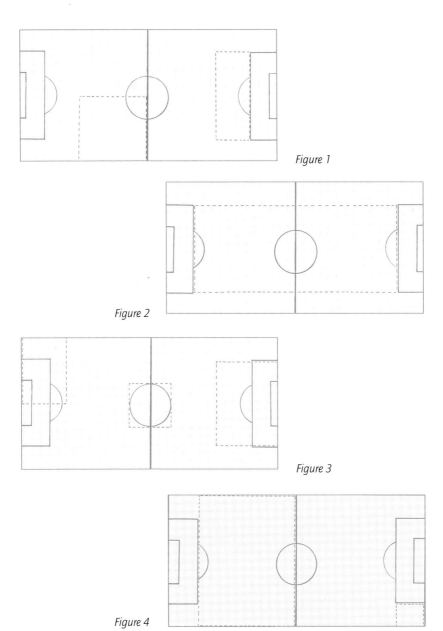

Figure 1

Figure 2

Figure 3

Figure 4

12 The Best Use of the "Play" Method for One's Own Training

As mentioned above, not all playing methods or variations can be adopted for all age groups or ability levels without question. Adjustments have to be made.

In order for the user to be able to recognize which groups are being addressed, the programmes are marked thus: ☒

Professional level:	Bundesliga/Regional Leagues
Amateur level:	Senior League/Association League/State league/ County A, B or C **Leagues:**
Junior level:	Junior As
Children and Youth levels:	Junior Bs and Cs

Note:
In various playing methods there can be overlaps between the groups. The Junior Ds, Es and Fs have not been considered in the Training sessions described in this book.

13 A Choice of Forty Different Training Sessions

About forty training weeks including preparation period have to be filled.
In the lower and middle grades, and at children's and teenagers' level, training usually takes place twice a week.

At Senior and Regional Leagues as well as in the Bundesliga there are two training sessions per training day (four to five training days).

This means that at amateur level one to two games per training session are enough. At professional level this can be increased to two or three ones.

The coach decides which points will receive emphasis in individual training sessions. There are five main areas of emphasis in soccer training:

1. Teaching defence (with the sweeper, four players in a line, with the sweeper in front of or behind the defence, tackling, offside traps, clearing).

2. Teaching attacking play (with three, two or one striker/s, playing on the wing and moving the centre of the game around the pitch).

3. Teaching attacking and defensive play (pressing, forechecking, playing with majority or minority).

4. Teaching physical fitness such as endurance, power, speed, flexibility and coordination.

5. Teaching technical skills (individual techniques, group skills, etc.).

Note:
Goalkeeper training can be carried out on an individual basis or in some cases with the team.

14 The Most Suitable Playing System

The question of a suitable playing system is very difficult to answer, as it is not the "system" that is of top priority in tactical considerations, but primarily the potential of every available player. The deciding criterion for a team's playing style is the lack of homogeneity in the composition of a team of individualists, which must first learn to adjust to a common tactical plan.

Every coach must therefore analyse his team in order to determine what sorts of players it is made up of. In this context not only the so called "regulars" have to be assessed but also the rest of the squad.

The cooperation between technically skilled, physically robust, tactically sophisticated and professionally-minded players, all finely tuned as a team, results in the actual "playing system".

The tactical orientation of the game is a result of the components of the objectives on the one hand, and of the situation at any given moment during and around the game on the other hand.

The score of the game, the advantages for the "home" team of playing on its own ground, public support etc., demand a specific fine tuning of the team by the coach.

15 Modern Playing Systems

Even tactical playing systems are frequently not immune to current trends, demonstrated initially by leading European or South American clubs and which are then imitated without question by even the smallest amateur clubs.

Frequently such trends originate not due to any influence by the coach but rather from a fortunate composition of the team. A so-called "player type" is born and is immediately regarded as the "non plus ultra".

16 Current Trends

The Brazilian System (World Cup 1994 in the USA)

In the 1994 World Cup the Brazilians favoured tactical playing which showed the team to be a compact unit, both in defence and in attack (see Fig. 5).

In defence a chain of four players plays together with four marking players in a line. When attacking the whole team is moving all the time, with and without the ball.
At the same time the buildup takes place over central positions and is then continued on the wings. An accurate short pass and a sudden pass into the centre of the game are a successful means of scoring a goal. When the team is loosing the ball the whole team withdraw just behind the centre line and moves in the direction of the ball in order to quickly regain possession of it.

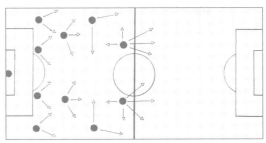

Fig. 5

The European System

In contrast to the Brazilian system, the European system functions - as it is practised in Germany among others - with a sweeper and two man marking players (the 3-5-2-system). The five midfield players share the remaining defensive tasks. As a rule there are two defensive players who do not concern themselves much with attacks (see Fig. 6). The attacks are determined by the three remaining midfield players, one of whom acts as a "Tail-End Charlie".

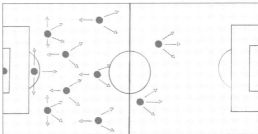

Fig. 6

The most important systems, as practised in the World Cup in the USA in 1994, are made clear in a simple graphic overview (see Figs. 7-13). They are so-called basic formations which are not used rigidly as such but which can be adjusted flexibly to the playing style of each opponent (after RUTEMÖLLER, E. in: "fußballtraining" (a periodical on soccer training), Vol. 6, 1996, published by Phillippka Verlag in Münster, Germany).

The Netherlands

The defence formation is formed by a chain of three players on a line. The midfield coordinates its play with three players, the two outer midfield players hold their positions and play as zone markers. The offensive strategy is marked by both outfield positions and an effective striker, who often move out to the wings. Long passes from the defence to both wings or to the front striker alternate with careful game buildup without gaining much ground.

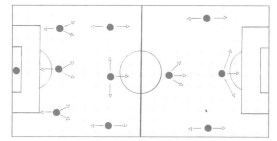

Fig. 7

Rumania

In the Rumanian defence a sweeper works behind two man marking defenders. Four midfielders play in the midfield, with the inside left often moving like a "windscreen-wiper" (i.e. back and forth) in front of his own sweeper.

The attack shows a front striker which stays at the centre line, even when the other team has possession of the ball. The two outside midfielders move into the attack from the wing again and again. The main feature of the strategy in this game are the counter moves, brought forward from a massed defence.

Fig. 8

Bulgaria

A sweeper plays behind the two man markers, but rarely gets involved in the Bulgarian attack. The midfield plays in a chain of four players, which puts up a defensive zone marking barrier against offensives from the opposing team. The offensive play is marked by play with three strikers in which the left striker often changes position but rarely helps out in the rear. The striker in the centre tends to play staying behind, and provides an opening for a midfielder moving up from the back .

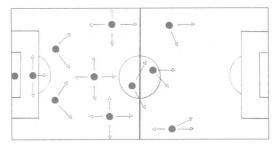

Fig. 9

Italy

The Italian team plays with a chain of four players in defence and two central midfielders in front of the defence, while the two others close the space leading to the outfield. The attack is started by the two offensive midfielders. A striker in front is supported by a striker who plays staying behind. The Italians prefer counter-attacking from a compact defence.

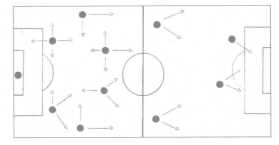

Fig. 10

Spain

In defence there is a Spanish sweeper who moves to the rear, away from both man markers. In the midfield there is a chain of three players, who, depending on the situation, give over the opposing players. Even the teams own striker often helps out in the rear.

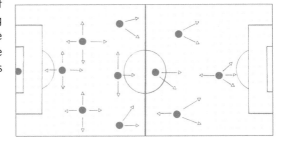

Fig. 11

25

The attack takes place mostly on the right. Both wingers hang back somewhat in contrast to the strikers and frequently change position with both outer midfielders. A resolute defence and quick change from defence to the attack, characterise Spanish soccer playing.

Switzerland

In defence the Swiss team play with a chain of four players in a line. Both inside players give over the opposing strikers. When attacking, two strikers - with a chain of four players standing behind them in midfield - play with the best player, who builds the game up mainly on the left-hand side of the field.

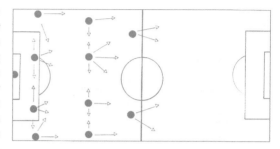

Fig. 12

Sweden

Swedish soccer players prefer a chain of four players in defence with every marker active in his own area. In the midfield a chain of four players mark the zone. The attack takes place mainly on the right-hand side of the midfield, which is an excellent way of bringing both strikers into the game. Both

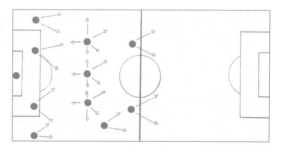

strikers like moving out to the wing, so that the left midfielder can move up.

Fig. 13

Conclusion:
Apart from the current trends favoured by national teams, top European teams and teams in the German Bundesliga, the coach has to analyse his team very carefully in order to develop the best tactical ploys.

Note: The players determine the system, not the coach!

17 Symbols

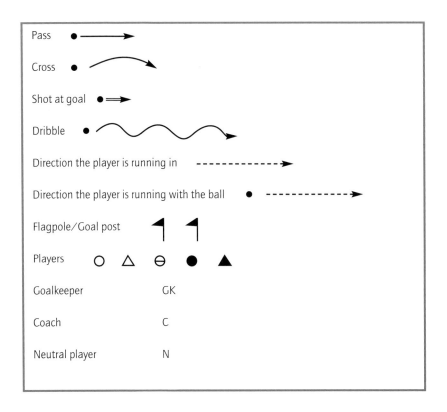

Pass	
Cross	
Shot at goal	
Dribble	
Direction the player is running in	
Direction the player is running with the ball	
Flagpole / Goal post	
Players	O △ ⊖ ● ▲
Goalkeeper	GK
Coach	C
Neutral player	N

18 Putting Theory into Practice

The practical section of this book does not represent an annual training timetable in the conventional sense. Rather, it is a collection of training units arranged in order of emphasis and which every coach can include in his total coaching plan. The training units presented here do not claim to be exhaustive.

In the chapter on **"Warm - up"** the coach is presented with 25 different stretching exercises and a corresponding **"Cool - down"** exercises.

19 The Training Units

1) Defensive play - man markers

2) Defensive play - midfield

3) Offside traps

4) Covering the midfield

5) Controlling the ball

6) Creating opportunities for scoring goals

7) Wall pass

8) Acting quickly - playing under pressure

9) Dribbling

10) Forechecking

11) Creating opportunities for scoring goals

12) Running behind the defence

13) Counterattack

14) Creativity in soccer game

15) The sweeper in front of the defence

16) The sweeper behind the defence

17) Changing quickly from defence to attack

18) Attacking play - playing on the wing

19) Attacking play - a means of countering a reinforced defence

20) Pressing

21) Marking zones

22) Fast playing

23) Moving back after losing the ball

24) Warm - up as a game

25) Teaching teamwork

26) Shot at goal from a dribble

27) Moving the centre of the game

28) Understanding the game

29) Playing through-passes

30) Playing goal-scoring

31) Creating apportunities for scoring goals

32) Majority game

33) Minority game

34) Moving to the ball

35) Free kick training

36) Corner kick training

37) Continuous kicking

38) Soccer tennis

39) Dribbling - Dribbling at speed

40) Passing to the striker

Note:
While performing the above exercises, the players also practise physical skills such as strength, endurance, speed and coordination which are included in the term "training objective".

☒ Professionals

☒ Amateurs

☒ Juniors

☒ Children / Teenagers

Objectives

"Pressing"-teaching defensive playing (man markers), and soccer-related endurance.

Didactic and methodical hints

- Adjusting distance and speed when running.
- Paying attention to feinting with the body.
- Paying attention to the position of the opponent (in front, behind and at the side).
- Making eye contact with a team-mate running next to oneself.
- Making deliberately false moves with one's own body to get the opponent out of his running or dribbling rhythm

Organisation

The players play 5:5 in one half of the field. Neither team attempts to score a goal. At the start of the game all players in one team are allocated a personal opponent in the opposing team whom they have to mark (see Fig. 14).

Fig. 14

Number of Players:	Ten.

Equipment: A ball, five bibs, marking cones.

Load: 5 x 5 minutes with complete recovery breaks (stretching).

Variation:
- Shortened playing time (more series).
- Extended playing time (less series).
- Limited ball contact (twice per player).
- Reduction in size of the playing field.
- Allocation of a new partner.
- "Press marking" only allowed in certain parts of the field.
- Let play at goals.

Note
The above game can also be practised as an exercise with a passer (errors can be corrected on an individual basis): A passer plays with an attacker against a man marker. The passer is only allowed to pass the ball directly to his partner (see Fig. 15).

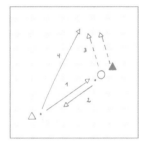

Fig. 15

When training children and teenagers, care should be taken to see that physical contact is not overdone. The correct position to the ball and to the opponents must be explained and corrected again and again.

☒ Professionals
☒ Amateurs
☒ Juniors
☒ Children/Teenagers

Objectives

Teaching defensive play to the midfielders, combined zone and man marking, quickness of start.

Didactic and methodical hints

- Occupying certain zones on the field and waiting for the opponents there.
- Establishing eye contact with one's nearest partner.
- Pursuing combination games or individual tactics on the part of the opposing team.
- "Pressing" of the opposing team in a given part of the field.
- Using running speed and escape routes, paying attention to feints and performing deceptive manoeuvres with one's body.
- When a "marked" opponent leaves the designated zone, not to follow him.

Organisation

The "5:3+2" Game

Five attacking players play against three midfielders and two defending players on a pitch half the size of a normal one. The goals are reduced in size accordingly.

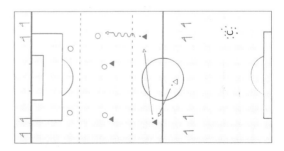

Fig. 16

32

The attackers start the game behind the centre line and try to keep the ball within their own lines in order to score a goal into one of the goals along the goal line.

The three midfielders take the attackers in a staked out-zone and "press". Both defence players behave passively, however.

When the "midfielders" have possession of the ball they can play towards the attackers' goal. If the "attackers" score a goal, however, the game starts again behind the centre line (see Fig. 16).

Number of players:	Ten.
Equipment:	Ten balls, ten coloured bibs, eight flag poles.
Load:	25 minutes with recovery breaks and stretching.
Variation:	– Reversal of roles between attackers and midfielders.
	– Each attacker is only allowed to come in contact with the ball twice.
	– The three midfielders follow their "marked" opponents when the latter change position.
	– The size of the pitch is increased.
	– The playing zone is extended as far as to the centre line.

Note

In order that the midfielders learn to run quickly into the previously determined playing zones, the attackers move in their half of the field via combination games while the midfielders run back and forth without the ball behind the centre line.

When the coach blows his whistle the players sprint into the marked "playing zone" (see Fig. 17). With children and teenagers the game should be repeatedly interrupted in order to correct any communication problems that arise.

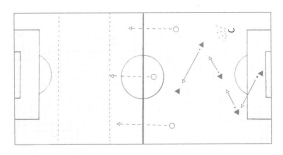

Fig. 17

⊠ Professionals

⊠ Amateurs

☐ Juniors

☐ Children/Teenagers

Objectives

Teaching the "offside trap" and teamwork between the defensive players (peripheral vision and timely acting on visual and acoustic signals).

Didactic methodical hints

– Establishing visual contact between the players.

– Setting offside traps only when the opposing strikers and midfielders have moved a long way into the other half of the field in order to receive the blocked ball again.

– The other players move forward rapidly after blocking the ball at the command of the defensive player (mostly the sweeper).

Organisation

6:5 Game

Six attackers start the buildup behind the centre line, moving the ball in one of three directions (1-3) as seen in Fig. 18. The attackers pass the ball (4) immediately towards the strikers (5). At the same moment that the ball is passed, all defensive players sprint to the front (6). After successfully setting the "offside trap", the attack from behind the centre line is renewed.

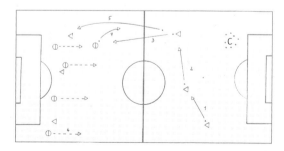

Fig. 18

Number of players:	Eleven.
Equipment:	Ten balls, six bibs.
Load:	25-30 minutes with short breaks and stretching.
Variation:	– Increasing the number of players (11:11).
	– Attacking and defensive players change roles.
	– Extending practice time.
	– The attacking players are only allowed two touches with the ball per player.

Note

The coach should draw this exercise on the blackboard and go through it orally with the players.

The "offside trap" can also be used in standard situations (free kicks and corner kicks).

The senior group of the Junior section can also be taught the "offside trap" .

☒ Professional

☒ Amateur

☒ Juniors

☐ Children/Teenagers

Objectives

"Rapid crossing" of the midfield and technically perfect through passes.

Didactic and methodical hints

- Well-practised buildup from the defence.
- Unmarked running and position changing by the strikers offer various passing opportunities.
- A through pass or a cross takes place when the opposing team has moved up from the rear.
- Quick, direct and disguised passes increase the speed of the game.
- A buildup through the outside/wing increases the effectiveness.

Organisation

Game 7:7 on the whole pitch.

The players play seven against seven on the whole field.

Both teams try to keep the ball in their own lines by practiced teamwork and to play a long volley pass over the marked "midfield zone" after the strikers well getting into space (see Fig. 19).

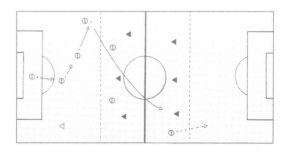

Fig. 19

Number of players:	Fourteen.
Equipment:	Five balls in each goal, bibs, marking cones.
Load:	3 x 20 minutes with short breaks and stretching.
Variation:	– Increasing the number of players to 11:11.
	– Two contacts per player in their own team's territory.
	– In the home zone only direct passes are allowed.
	– Let the teams play in minority or mayority.
	– Goals may only be scored after the ball has been dribbled.
	– The coach nominates a player who always has to pass the ball over the zone.
	– The goalkeeper joins the game.

Note

A goal is only worth double when the ball is kicked or passed as described above (this increases motivation).

Unit 5

☒ Professionals
☒ Amateurs
☒ Juniors
☐ Children/Teenagers

Objectives

"Saving" the ball within the players' own team, training in techniques as well as improving playing abilities and creativity.

Didactic and methodical hints

- Establishing eye-contact with other team members when in possession of the ball.
- Maintaining control of the ball while dribbling it with both feet.
- Maintaining control of the ball by shielding it from an opponent (the player's body is between the ball and an opponent).
- Coordinating running speed and ball-control.
- With increasing ball skills, being able to take one's eyes off the ball (this is for easier orientation on the field).
- Forcing diversions/feints at and with the ball.
- Getting team-mates to pass the ball in time.

Organisation

The team plays 5:5 in one half of the field using smaller goals.
The pitch is divided up into three identical sections. On pitch No. 1 the team with the ball has to keep it within its own lines as long as possible through dribbling and well practised teamwork.

Fig. 20

On pitch No. 2 the members of the team in possession of the ball may only touch the ball twice.
On pitch No. 3 the player with the ball is allowed to dribble it as long as he wishes in order to score a goal. (see Fig. 20).

Number of Players: Ten.

Equipment: A ball, five bibs, four goalposts.

Load: 3 x 10 minutes with short breaks and stretching.

Variation: – On field 1 + 2 retaining ball possession by dribbling, practised passing.
– Extension of the playing time.
– Dividing the playing field into two identical sections only.

Note

The above game can be carried out as a competition in order to see which team can retain possession of the ball the longest time.

☒ Professionals

☒ Amateurs

☒ Juniors

☒ Children/Teenagers

Objectives

Creating opportunities for scoring goals, improving teamwork between team members, soccer-related endurance.

Didactic and methodical hints

- Skilful presentation and getting into space.
- Occupying various zones on the field evenly (using the whole playing field).
- Awareness of staggering when the opposing team has possession of the ball.
- Acting quickly when near the penalty area (try to score a goal).
- Calling for communication between team members (giving instructions and support).

Organisation

The players play 6:6:6 with rapid goal scoring.

Three teams with six players each line up, as shown in Fig. 21. Team A stands in the penalty area, Team B stands in the opposite penalty area and Team C stands on the centre line.

Team C starts an attack at the centre line against Team A and tries to score a goal. After a goal has been scored the ball ends up "out" or lost to the other team, Teams A and C change positions and Team A now plays against Team B and so on.

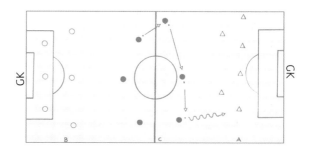

Fig. 21

Number of players:	Twenty (eighteen players and two goalkeepers).
Equipment:	Several balls, six green, red and yellow bibs.
Load:	4 x 10 minutes playing with short breaks and stretching.
Variation:	– Limited ball contact for each player.

– Limited ball contact for each player.
– Reduction of the number of players (4:4:4).
– A goal must be scored within a certain period determined by the coach or the team loses the ball.
– Shots are only allowed in a certain part of the pitch e.g. only outside the penalty area.
– Playing time is extended (insert longer break periods e.g. jogging).
– Playing time is reduced.

Note
The above game may be treated as a competition to see who can score the most goals.

☒ Professionals

☒ Amateurs

☒ Juniors

☒ Children/Teenagers

Objectives

"Wall Passing Game", aerobic and anaerobic endurance and precise playing.

Didactic and methodical hints

− Encourage players to evade players from the other team quickly after the pass.
− Make sure the players spread out properly on the field and do not get in the way of their team-mates.
− Make sure the players keep going for the ball in open spaces.
− Create a majority of players when one's own team has possession of the ball.
− Demand precise passing.

Organisation

The players play the "6:6+2 Neutrals" game on one half of the playing field using two goals.

Two teams play into two goals with support from two "neutral" players at the same time. The "neutrals" always play with the team in possession of the ball, but are only allowed to pass the ball directly. The remaining players are only allowed two contacts with the ball each.

Goals only count after a wall pass (see Fig. 22).

Fig. 22

Number of players:	Fourteen (12 players + 2 "neutrals").
Equipment:	Several balls, six green and two red bibs, two flag poles.
Load:	5 x 5 minutes with short breaks and running around.
Variation:	– Shots at goal are allowed after receiving a direct pass or a cross.
	– Increase the number of "neutrals".
	– Increase playing time (reducing the number of series and increasing of rest time).
	– Reduce playing time (increasing the number of series).
	– The "neutrals" are allowed to dribble the ball.
	– Reducing the size of the pitch (putting the players under pressure).

Note

The coach should correct faults by stopping play.

This form of game involves a lot of running and hence requires well rested players.

☒ Professionals

☒ Amateurs

☒ Juniors

☐ Children/Teenagers

Objectives

"Fast playing" i.e. playing under pressure in terms of time and available space on the pitch. Soccer - related endurance.

Didactic and methodical hints

– Ensure a quick grasp of the situation on the pitch through inner motivation.
– Demand rapid switch from defence to attack.
– Safe staggering of the players when on the defence area.
– Reduce the distance between players in the defence area.
– The team spreads out in a fan-shaped pattern after gaining possession of the ball.
– Forming a majority of players around the ball.
– A hidden pass towards the strikers.
– Demand quick and safe 1:1 dribbling.

Organisation

Game 8:8+ 1 "neutral" goalkeeper.
Two groups play from one penalty area to the other, each with two small goals.
A goalkeeper stands in the centre-circle, to whom both teams may kick the ball.

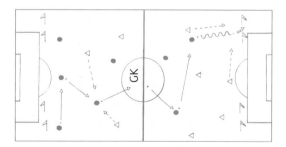

Fig. 23

44

The goal keeper passes the ball on with a targeted throw so that the team in possession of the ball can score a goal (see Fig. 23).

Number of players: Seventeen (16 players + 1 goalkeeper).

Equipment: Several balls, eight coloured bibs, eight flag poles.

Load: 2 X 20 minutes with a short break and stretching exercises.

Variation:
- Shorten playing time (increasing the number of series).
- The goalie is replaced by an outfield player who has to pass the ball with his feet.
- Set a fixed time in which a goal must be scored, otherwise the other team is given possession of the ball.
- Limit the number of ball contacts.
- Increase the number of players in order to generate more pressure (playing space is reduced).

Note

This form of playing must be carried out after the "warm-up" as it involves a lot of running and requires mental agility on the part of the players.

☒ Professionals
☒ Amateurs
☒ Juniors
☐ Children/Teenagers

Objectives

"Dribbling" - consolidating dribbling techniques, feinting and other deceptive manoeuvres (tricks), soccer-related endurance.

Didactic and methodical hints

– Feinting while running and by using the body, both without the ball in order to gain possession of the ball.
– Require short passes and rapid shaking-off of the opponents.
– Always conclude a dribbling with a shot at goal.
– Require the players to dribble with both feet.
– The players should not lose eye contact with other team members.
– Look for a chance to tackle an opposing player.

Organisation

The players play 2:2 towards two goals with two "neutrals" and two goalkeepers. Three teams of two players play alternately against each other on a section of the pitch extending beyond the penalty area. The team resting stands sideways to the penalty area and act as a "neutral" passing point. After a given time the players change (see Fig. 24).

Fig. 24

46

Number of Players:	Six players and two goalkeepers.
Equipment:	Two large goals, several balls, six different coloured bibs.
Load:	10 x 2 minutes.
Variation:	– Increase the number of players, thereby reducing the playing space.
	– Reduce playing time (increasing of series).
	– Extend playing time (reducing the number of series and extending break times).
	– Goalkeepers may only defend their goals with their feet (higher score rate).
	– The two resting players can jog round the pitch as a recovery break.

Note

If this type of exercise is carried out at the end of a training session, it does not lead to any improvement in dribbling techniques but only to a strength endurance load which approximately simulates the load situation at the 80th minute of a game.

☒ Professionals
☒ Amateurs
☒ Juniors
☐ Children/Teenagers

Objectives

"Forechecking", or pushing the opposing team back into its half of the pitch or the penalty area.

Didactic and methodical hints

- Technically weak teams can be easily pushed back into their own half of the pitch.
- Aggressive foiling of the other team's defence causes them to make mistakes and prevents them from building up an effective attack.
- Strikers and attacking midfielders are best able to obstruct the opposing team.
- The rest of the team has to move up in order to keep up with those team members at the front.
- Forechecking cannot be used over 90 minutes, as this overtaxes the players.
- All players should act in a coordinated fashion and not just attack the ball controlling player, but also those opposing players without the ball.

Organisation

Game 6:4 + 1 goalkeeper on one half of the pitch with one large and two small goals.
One team of six players the other team of four and the goal keeper.
The team with six players tries immediately to obstruct its opponents once the latter have gained possession of the ball.

Fig. 25

48

The team with four members tries to score a goal in the smaller goals through buildup-tactics and teamwork.

After a goal has been scored, the game continues by the goalie's throw-out.

The team with six members is only allowed to carry out its "forechecking" tactics in the penalty area (see fig. 25).

Number of Players:	Eleven (10 players and one goalkeeper).
Equipment:	Several balls, six red and four green bibs, four flag poles.
Load:	3 x 15 minutes with short breaks and stretching exercises.
Variation:	– Extend the forechecking zone.
	– Increase the number of players on both sides.
	– Increase the number of players on the defending side.
	– Shorten playing time (increasing of series).
	– Increase playing time (reducing of series and extending of recovery phases).
	– Set a fixed time for „forechecking", this starts and finishes on a command from the coach.
	– Game 11:11; both teams are required to carry out "forechecking".
	– The teams swap roles after 15 minutes.

Note

As forechecking requires much strength and running, this exercise should be used at the end of a training unit. Indvidual training in technique can be done before this.

Unit 11

☒ Professionals
☒ Amateurs
☒ Juniors
☐ Children/Teenagers

Objectives

"Creating" goal opportunities, soccer related endurance, acceleration speed with and without the ball.

Didactic and methodical hints

– Ensure that the players are equally spread out around the pitch.
– Taking a pass from the man with the ball before the opposing team does it.
– Ensuring possession of the ball when the players are closer together in front of the goal; setting up a new attack.
– Looking for a quick shot at goal, including by way of unexpected shots.
– Deliberately passing the ball to the "neutral" player.
– Demand fast play.

Organisation

Game 6:6 on one half of the pitch with two goals.
The player's job is to attempt a goal as quickly as possible. Both "neutral" players are only allowed to pass the ball on directly to another player (see Fig. 26).

Fig. 26

50

Number of Players:	Fourteen (12 players + 2 goalkeepers).
Equipment:	One ball, two large goals, six red bibs and two green bibs ("neutrals").
Load:	5 x 5 minutes with short breaks and stretching exercises.
Variation:	– Extending the time of the game (reducing of series and extending of breaks).
	– Increasing of series (time reducing with longer breaks).
	– Change the "neutral" players after five minutes.
	– Goals scored by heading the ball count double.
	– Only certain players, previously nominated by the coach, are allowed to score goals.
	– Increase the number of "neutral" players.
	– Limit ball contacts between the players.
	– Set a time limit in which the team in possession of the ball has to shoot at the goal.
	– Divide the players into three groups of six. Two teams play each other and the other team has a break by jogging round the pitch (aerobic endurance).

Note

This form of exercise is particularly suitable for training the midfielders and both strikers separately, who will play together in a match. Coordination problems can get rid of.

☒ Professionals

☒ Amateurs

☒ Juniors

☐ Children/Teenagers

Objectives

Running behind the opposing team's defence, soccer-related endurance, sprint speed.

Didactic and methodical hints

– Skilled distribution of players over the pitch at the own buildup of an attack.
– The players establish eye contact with each other.
– Each team tries to control the ball in order to give its quick players the opportunity of running behind the opposition's defence.
– Unexpectedly passing into the space.
– Sprinting in order to break up the opposing defence and to get behind it.
– Running behind the opposing defence can be started by the strikers crossing in front of the opposing defence.
– This is only useful when the other team is acting with zone marking.
– Mind the opponents' "offside-trap".

Organisation

The players play 8:8 from penalty area to penalty area, each with two small goals and a zone approximately 10 m wide and divided up on both sides.

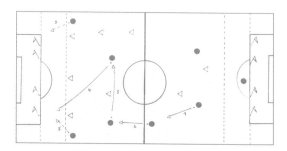

Fig. 27

Through expert teamwork of the ball possessing team, two players wearing differently coloured bibs have to try to run behind the opposing defence and get into the marked "zone".
A goal can only be scored by the two players inside the "zone" (see Fig. 27).

Number of Players: Sixteen.

Equipment: Several balls, eight goal posts, eight cones, six green and two yellow bibs (for the runners).

Load: 3 x 15 minutes sessions with short breaks and stretching exercises.

Variation:
    – Reduce the number of players (6:6).
    – Increase the size of the playing pitch to make it easier to run behind the defending team.
    – Let play to large goals with two goalkeepers.
    – Increase playing time (reducing of series).
    – Reduce playing time (increasing of series).
    – Several players can run behind the opposition defence.
    – Change the "runners" more often.
    – Extend the size of each zone in order to make it easier to run behind the opposition defence.

Note
This form of training involves a lot of running and sprinting, especially for the two "runners". For this reason it should be carried out only with mentally and physically fresh players.

☒ Professionals
☒ Amateurs
☒ Juniors
☐ Children/Teenagers

Objectives

"Counterattacks" as a means of attacking quickly and scoring a goal, sprint speed, exploiting a counterattack, speed endurance.

Didactic and methodical hints

- Counterattacking is only practical when all members of the opposing team have moved forward and are not positioned orderly (i.e. are not positioned from the front to the rear of the team).
- Each team practises safe short passes within its own lines until the counterattack starts.
- The defending team regains possession of the ball, spreads out on the pitch and team members call for passes.
- Get the players to make exact through passes to the strikers.
- Ensure that the countering team moves forward quickly.
- Take a risk when attempting a shot at goal.

Organisation

The players play 6:6 with a goalkeeper, one large goal and two small goals, both of which are positioned 10 m behind the centre line.

After gaining possession of the ball, Team A tries to start a quick counterattack in the direction of the two small goals.

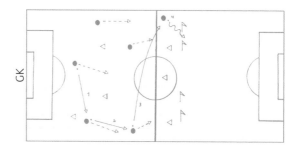

Fig. 28

After Team B has gained possession of the ball and Team A has moved foward, Team B also attempts a counterattack on the large goal (see Fig. 28).

Number of Players: Twelve players and a goalkeeper.

Equipment: Several balls, six coloured bibs and four flag poles.

Load: 3 x 15 minutes sessions with short breaks and cool-down.

Variation:
− Enlarge the playing pitch (the players have to run longer distances but counterattacking is made easier).
− Increase the number of players to 11 on each side.
− Each player of the countering team may only have two ball contacts.
− Increase playing time (reducing of series, longer recovery breaks).
− Designate one "neutral" player per team who has to do the countering (this encourages the best player).

Note
Recovery breaks can be carried out with active use of the ball, e.g. individual technique work, "soccer tennis" or games of 5:2 etc.

⊠ Professionals

⊠ Amateurs

⊠ Juniors

⊠ Children/Teenagers

Objectives

"Playing creativity" - forced development of individual techniques, soccer-related endurance.

Didactic and methodical hints

– Dribble the ball as often as possible.

– Close ball control with both feet.

– Looking up while playing the ball.

– Maintaining eye contact with other players.

– Looking for tackling opportunities (1:1; 1:2).

– Trying out new tricks and feints.

– Forcing the players to make a final shot at goal after a successfull dribbling.

Organisation

Play 6:6 in the penalty area using small goals (Youth Size) with the objective of successfull dribbling, and "tricking" the opposing players.

Two teams attempt to score a goal as quickly as possible by clever dribbling within the penalty area.

If the ball goes over the penalty lines, the coach immediately throws another ball into the game so that the game can continue without break (see Fig. 29).

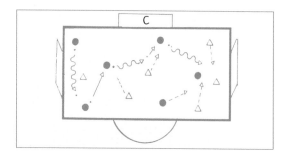

Fig. 29

Number of Players:	Twelve.
Equipment:	All the balls, six coloured bibs, two youth sized goals or four goal posts.
Load:	3 X 15 minutes with short breaks and stretching.
Variation:	– Increase the number of players (so that they play under more pressure).
	– Reducing of playing time (increasing of series).
	– Form several teams so that the game can be played in tournament fashion.
	– Form three teams. Two teams play and one has a break by jogging round the pitch or it practises techniques with the ball (every player has a ball).

Note
Controlling the ball within the penalty area is well suited as a means of warming up for this training session. Every player needs a ball for this.

☒ Professionals

☒ Amateurs

☒ Juniors

☐ Children/Teenagers

Objectives

Coaching "sweeper" tactics in front of the defence as an additional element of the attack.

Didactic and methodical hints

- Check the position to both man markers constantly.
- Establish eye contact with the players in the forward lines.
- Fill the spaces on the right and the left of the pitch (defensive tactics).
- Indicate constantly to your own goalkeeper that he can pass the ball to you.
- After receiving the ball start your own buildup through the outside midfielders immediately.
- Force wall passes through the middle of the pitch.
- Look for the opportunity to bring the action to a close directly adjacent to the penalty area.
- If you lose possession of the ball, move immediately back into the main lines of the team or start forechecking with the opposing team.

Organisation

Play 5:5 with a goalkeeper on one half of the pitch using one large goal and two small ones on the centre line. Two teams play against each other; the sweeper's job is to play in front of the defence and to join in his own team's buildup (see Fig. 30).

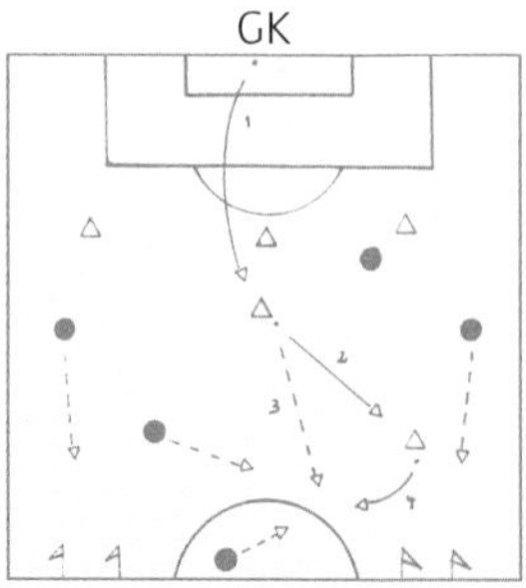

Fig. 30

Number of Players:	Ten players and one goalkeeper.
Equipment:	One ball, four green bibs and one yellow one (sweeper), four flag poles.
Load:	25 minutes.
Variation:	– Increase the number of players, (dense space for the sweeper).
	– Increase the area of the playing pitch, thus making things easier for the sweeper.
	– The sweeper may only have two ball contacts with each player.
	– Every player takes a turn at playing sweeper.
	– Every goal scored by the sweeper counts double.
	– Play 11:11 on the whole pitch for 35 minutes.

Note

Exercises with an offensive playing sweeper at the front of the team require extremely disciplined acting of the other defensive and marking players when cordoning him off. The midfielders are primarily responsible for immediately closing the resulting gap by withdrawing or changing position.

$\boxtimes$ Professionals

$\boxtimes$ Amateurs

$\boxtimes$ Juniors

$\square$ Children/Teenagers

Objectives

Coaching the sweeper game behind the defence, as organiser of the entire defence.

Didactic and methodical hints

- Establish eye contact with the goalkeeper, man-to-man markers and defensive midfield players.
- Give team-mates positioning instructions in standard situations (free kick, corner kick, throw-in).
- Observe own positional play in order to always keep well away from the players in front.
- Fill the spaces to meet opposing forwards who have run through.
- Carry out clearance kicks to free own defence from opposing pressure.
- Give the signal for setting up an "offside trap".
- Don't feel tempted to move too far out of the centre of defence.
- Skilful involvement in own team's buildup after goal kick, bounces and defence actions.

Organisation

Play 6:6 on half a normal playing field with two small goals each on the base line and also on the centre line.

Two teams play against each other, the sweeper has the job of always getting away from the players in front to direct the entire defence group. When his own team has possession of the ball, he gives the command to move up quickly. He can join in his team's buildup without crossing the centre line (see Fig. 31).

Fig. 31

Number of Players:	Twelve.
Equipment:	One ball, five green bibs and one yellow one (sweeper), eight goal poles.
Load:	30 minutes.
Variation:	– Increase the number of players, thereby increasing pressure from the opponent.
	– Play with three opposing forwards thus forcing the sweeper to run to the wings to fill "holes".
	The coach whistles selectively for free kicks to teach correct action of the sweeper.
	– Each player takes a turn at being sweeper.
	– Form three teams of six players: two teams play against each other and the third one rests with easy ball work.

Note

The role of sweeper should be assigned to an experienced player who can use both feet and has good positional and heading skills. Calm, easy-going players seem to be especially suited to this position. In children's and adolescent training this exercise can only be carried out in a simpler form.

☒ Professionals

☒ Amateurs

☒ Juniors

☐ Children/Teenagers

Objectives

Coaching the rapid change from defensive to attacking play, fast sprinting with and without the ball.

Didactic and methodical hints

– Getting away from the opposing player quickly after gaining possession of the ball.
– Making an accurate short pass while moving forward.
– The midfielders run to the sidelines in order to create several passing points for the ball controlling player.
– Surprise the opposing players, who have moved forward with through passes to the strikers.
– Force rapid wall passes and look for opportunities to score a goal.

Organisation

Play 6:6 with two goalkeepers in an area 3/4 of the size of the normal pitch. After gaining possession of the ball, the defending team must attempt to score a goal by rapid teamwork, skilful free running and offering passing points. The ball possessing defenders who are moving forward have to run as fast as possible through a marked "zone".

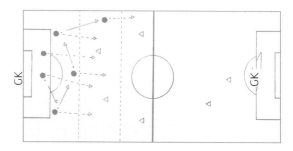

Fig. 32

Number of Players: Fourteen (12 players + 2 goalkeepers).

Equipment: Several balls, six coloured bibs, two large goals and marking cones for the "zone".

Load: 3 x 15 minutes with short breaks and stretching exercises.

Variation:
- Increase the number of players, thereby increasing space density for the team moving forward.
- Increase playing time (reducing of series).
- After 15 minutes the teams change roles.
- Form several teams: two teams play against each other while the rest is practising technique training.

Note
The coach steps in if necessary to rectify any mistakes e.g. if anybody makes mistakes in running clear or has bad positional play in defence.

☒ Professionals
☒ Amateurs
☒ Juniors
☐ Children/Teenagers

Objectives

Forcing offensive play over the wings, soccer-related endurance and individual techniques.

Didactic and methodical hints

- Create a majority of players in the own buildup.
- Running clear of the midfielders.
- Quick passes to those players posted on the wings.
- Opening of the space along the sideline for players moving forward.
- Starting solos along the sideline.
- Create one-on-one situations with break-through towards the goal line.
- Aim crosses to the near or far goal post, or far beyond the five metre space.
- Low back pass from the goal line behind the defending team.
- Long diagonal passes towards the wings.
- Through passes towards the wingers.

Organisation

Play 7:7 with two goalkeepers on the whole pitch.

By skilful buildup, two teams attempt to bring the players on the wings into play (through both of the flag poles on each half of the pitch).

These players dribble the ball in an attempt to break through to the goal line in order to pass the ball back behind the oppenent or to cross it (see Fig. 33).

Fig. 33

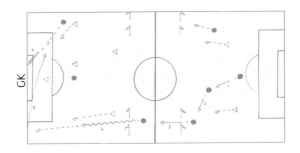

Number of Players: Fourteen players and two goalkeepers.

Equipment: Several balls, eight flag poles, seven coloured bibs.

Load: 3 x 20 minutes with short breaks and stretching.

Variation:
 – Increase the number of players (11:11).
 – Limit ball contact within each team's own half to two per player.
 – Reduce the number of players by forming several teams.
 – Goals count double when scored after a cross or a header.
 – Both wingers in each team run up and down around the centre line until they get a through pass (game 5+2 wingers). Only then do they step in to the game.

Note
In cases of weak crosses, special cross training is strongly recommended.

☒ Professionals
☒ Amateurs
☒ Juniors
☒ Children/Teenagers

Objectives

"Offensive" playing versus a reinforced defence, soccer-related endurance, fast start off, ball-skills.

Didactic and methodical hints

– Good distribution in the opposing team's area.
– Get players to occupy the wings.
– Crossing of the strikers in front of the opposing defence zone.
– Demand a high running performance from those players without the ball.
– Demand proper staggering from the midfielders.
– Create penalty area situations by changing positions.
– Back passes from the front to the rear space.
– Skilled short passes.
– Strikes on the goal from the second row.
– Consciously have three strikers attack.

Organisation

Play 5:6 + 1 goalkeeper on one half of the pitch using the normal goal and two small ones on the centre line.

One team begins its attack at the centre line and attempts to score a goal in the face of a massive defence.

After scoring a goal, or after the ball has been kicked out, another attack starts at the centre line. After gaining possession of the ball, the defending team can try to score a goal in one of the two small goals (see Fig. 34).

Fig. 34

66

Number of Players:	Twelve (11 players + 1 goalkeeper).
Equipment:	Several balls, six coloured bibs and four flag poles.
Load:	3 x 15 minutes with short breaks and stretching/cool-down.
Variation:	– Increase the number of players in defence, thereby increasing space density on the pitch.
	– Extention of playing time (reducing of the number of series).
	– The defending team is only allowed to block the ball directly without its own buildup.
	– Reversal of roles.
	– Form several teams (at least three), two of whom play against each other while the other one rests.
	– Each player of the attacking team may only have two touches of the ball.

Note

As this form of play requires a lot of running at sprint speed, the strikers should be changed more often.

☒ Professionals
☒ Amateurs
☒ Juniors
☐ Children/Teenagers

Objectives

Using "pressing" as a means of early attacking the opponent and putting him under pressure; soccer-related endurance and fast start off.

Didactic and methodical hints

– Skilful distribution when the opposing team is in possession of the ball.
– At least two players always attack the ball controlling player.
– The players move in the direction of the ball and press at speed.
– Aim at majority near to the ball.
– Pressing cannot be used all the time as it requires a lot of effort in running and tackling.
– Pressing should only be used when the ball controlling player does not yet have orientation, or just before he stops and controls the ball.
– Pressing usually takes place 10 m in front of or behind the centre line.

Organisation

Play 4:6 + 1 goalkeeper in one half of the pitch using one large and two small goals.

The team with the minority begins to play from the centre line in the direction of the large goal.

The team with the majority has to keep trying to attack the ball controlling player with two of its own players.

When the other team gains possession of the ball, it can try to score a goal in one of the two goals on the centre line (Fig. 35).

Fig. 35

68

Number of Players:	Ten players and one goalkeeper.
Equipment:	Several balls, six coloured bibs and four flag poles.
Load:	3 x 10 minutes with short breaks and stretching.
Variation:	– Increase the number of players (11:11). – After a successful pressing and possession of the ball, the buildup starts from the centre line again. – Lengthen playing time, thereby reducing of the number of series.

Note

At the start of the practice session it is useful that the coach gives the command for the pressing.

☒ Professionals
☒ Amateurs
☒ Juniors
☐ Children/Teenagers

Objectives

Zone marking - training of the right strategy, soccer-related endurance.

Didactic and methodical hints

– If a team ends up in a numerical minority it has to play with zone marking.
– Moving to the side of the ball in good time.
– Maintain eye contact with each other.
– Staggering must be set up in an overlapping defence.
– Don't follow an opponent player with zone marking, but hand him over.
– Give the players verbal support.
– Near the penalty area zone marking must turn into man-to-man marking.
– Zone marking is economic because of short running distances.

Organisation

Play 5:6 in one half of the pitch using two small goals on the sidelines.
The team with majority should use the whole width of the pitch in order to force the other (smaller) team to move to one side (see Fig. 36).

Fig. 36

Number of Players:	Eleven.
Equipment:	Several balls, six coloured bibs and eight flag poles.
Load:	5 x 5 minutes with short breaks and stretching.
Variation:	– Increase the number of series (extending of breaks by active ball work).
	– Players should only play zone marking from a given zone.
	– Increase playing time (reduction of series).
	– Increase the number of players to 11:11.

Note

Zone marking demands a high degree of alertness and intelligence for playing from all team-members, and therefore requires intensive training.

☒ Professionals
☒ Amateurs
☒ Juniors
☐ Children/Teenagers

Objectives

"Playing speed" – high-speed teamwork, ball skills, soccer-related endurance and sprinting speed.

Didactic and methodical hints

– Require fast getting into space.
– Aim at repeated quick wall passes.
– Create numerical majority at the ball in order to gain possession of it as quickly as possible.
– Aim for skilful teamwork (wall passes).
– Get the players to use both feet in order to create surprising effects e.g. hidden passes.

Organisation

Play 5:5 with no goals in one half of the pitch. Two teams play against each other without scoring a goal, both with no more than two ball contacts per player (see Fig. 37).

Fig. 37

Number of Players: Ten.

Equipment: One ball, five coloured bibs.

Load: 5 x 5 minutes with short breaks and recovery runs.

Variation: – Reduced ball contact (direct passes) means the players have to run more.
– Increasing of ball contact (three or more).
– Increasing of the number of players. This means less ball contact per player.
– Reduction of playing time (increase of series).
– Let play majority. The smaller team has no restrictions in playing.
– Form several teams (at least three) which play against each other (those not playing have a rest and jog around).

Note
As this form of playing involves a lot of running and sprinting, it should first be preceded by a good "warm-up" session.

☒Professionals

☒ Amateurs

☒ Juniors

☒ Children

Objectives

Drawing back after losing possession of the ball, soccer-related endurance.

Didactic and methodical hints

– Drawing back is only useful when the opposing team is lined up, shows a good buildup or where regaining possession of the ball through "forechecking" does not seem a good idea.
– Rapid orientation on the pitch after own's losing possession of the ball in the opponent's half.
– Running back quickly to previously determined positions.
– Make spaces smaller by majority in one's own half of the pitch.

Organisation

Play 7:7 from penalty area to penalty area using two large goals.
After losing posession of the ball the players try to run as fast as possible to pre-determined positions in their own half of the pitch (see Fig. 38).

Fig. 38

Number of Players:	Fourteen players and two goalkeepers.
Equipment:	One ball, seven coloured bibs, two large goals.
Load:	3 x 15 minutes with short breaks and stretching.
Variation:	– Increase the number of players (11:11).
	– All players, including both spearhead attackers, have to draw back behind the centre line.
	– Reduce the number of series, thereby extension of playing time.
	– Form three teams. Two play against each other while the third has a rest with active ball exercises.

Note

At the beginning of the training unit the coach gives the command for drawing back in time.

☒ Professionals

☒ Amateurs

☒ Juniors

☒ Children/Teenagers

Objectives

Playing warm up, improving of technique, improvisation and creativity with the ball.

Didactic and methodical hints

- Every player must have a ball.
- Demand two-footed ball control.
- Demand for gaining space with the ball.
- Take your eyes off the ball.
- Use feints and diversions with the body against an imaginary opponent.
- Try out new tricks: step over manoeuvres, the Okocha trick, the Beckenbauer twist, sole trick, the Stan Mathews trick etc.
- Demand for juggling the ball on the spot and while moving.

Organisation

Each player has a ball and is in the penalty area. There is a 25 x 30 m playing pitch behind the centre line.

The players move with the ball and practise individually.

On command from the coach all players change with the ball into the other half of the pitch and continue to play there (see Fig. 39).

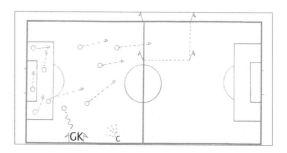

Fig. 39

Number of Players:	All players.
Equipment:	All the balls, bench seats, flag poles, marker cones, soccer bibs of various colours.
Load:	25-30 minutes with short breaks and stretching.
Variation:	– Distraction of each other when controlling the ball.
	– On command sprinting with the ball into the other pitch .
	– Only the players in the green bibs have to change pitches.
	– Only the players in the yellow bibs have to control the ball with their "weak" foot.
	– Only the players in the red bibs may juggle the ball.
	– Only those players called by the coach may dribble the ball and shoot at goal, towards a goalkeeper standing on one side (see fig. 39).

Note

Improvement of technique can best be organised in circle or station training. The players can improve specific techniques, feints and other tricks at these stations.

⊠ Professionals
⊠ Amateurs
⊠ Juniors
☐ Children/Teenagers

Objectives

Teaching "teamwork", aerobic endurance and individual techniques.

Didactic and methodical hints

 − Skilled covering of the pitch.
 − Get into space towards the man with the ball.
 − Accurate, short passes directly to a team-mate's feet.
 − Demand for space gaining dribbling.
 − Hidden passes with established eye contact with a team mate.
 − Pass the ball accurately into the "zone" at the other end of the pitch.

Organisation

Play 6:6 in an area 3/4 the size of the soccer pitch with an extended "zone" in both penalty areas.

Using skilled teamwork the ball possessing team tries to make a final pass into the "zone", which a player has to get while running.

Each of such passes counts as one point. Then the other team tries to make a pass into the "zone" etc. A player may only enter the "zone" at the moment of the pass (see Fig. 40).

Fig. 40

Number of Players:	Twelve.
Equipment:	Several balls, four markers and six coloured bibs.
Load:	3 X 15 minutes with short breaks.
Variation:	– Increase of the number of players (higher density on the pitch).
	– Each team has one player who runs up and down in the "zone" and who can receive passes.
	– Increase playing time (reduction of series).

Note
Precise passing can also be carried out in a special training with a partner.

Unit 26

☒ Professionals

☒ Amateurs

☒ Juniors

☒ Children/Teenagers

Objectives

    Scoring a goal from a dribble (one-on-one with the goalie), precise teamwork, soccer-related endurance.

Didactic and methodical hints

    – Quick reaction to an acoustic signal or a call.
    – Immediate control of the ball.
    – Quick and short movements.
    – Overrun of the opponent by sprinting.
    – Controlled shot at goal.

Organisation

    Six pairs of players move in a marked section of the pitch right next to the penalty area and pass the ball to each other. On command of the coach one pair changes to one-on-one play with strike at goal (see Fig. 41).

Fig. 41

Number of Players: Twelve players and a goalkeeper.

Equipment: Six balls and four flag poles.

Load: 20 minutes.

Variation: – Three players pass the ball to each other (2:1 + a goalkeeper).
– The coach gives the command to each pair two consecutive times (strength endurance).
– Longer breaks should be planned here.

Note

The 1:1 play makes high demands on the players' strength endurance and should not be followed by speed training.

☒Professionals

☒ Amateurs

☐ Juniors

☐ Children/Teenagers

Objectives

Moving the centre of play, soccer-related endurance, making long passes.

Didactic and methodical hints

– Accurate buildup in one's own half of the pitch.
– Forcing the opponents to the area of the ball using short passes.
– Hidden through passes to the other side of the pitch.
– The player in the corridor must keep moving in order to receive the through pass.
– The player in the corridor tries a shot at goal immediately after bringing down the ball.

Organisation

Play 7:7 with two goalkeepers on the normal goals with a corridor marked out along to the sideline. A player from each team moves up and down in each corridor of the attacking half of his team. Using clever teamwork and moving the centre of play the ball controlling team tries to get clear the player in the corridor. This player attacks the opponents' goal (see Fig. 42).

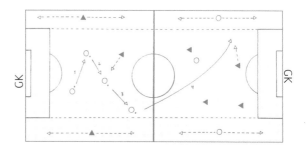

Fig. 42

Number of Players:	Fourteen players + two goalkeepers.
Equipment:	Several balls, seven coloured bibs, four marker cones.
Load:	3 x 15 minutes with short breaks to be used for jogging exercises.
Variation:	– Limit the number of contacts between players to two per player.
	– Limit the number of contacts between players only in their own half of the pitch.
	– Increase the number of players on the pitch (11:11).
	– Reduce the number of series, whilst extending playing time.

Note

The player in each corridor should be changed frequently.

In the upper junior level this form of training can also be combined with easier tasks.

☒Professionals

☒ Amateurs

☒ Juniors

☐ Children/Teenagers

Objectives

Understanding the game, soccer-related endurance, individual techniques.

Didactic and methodical hints

- Organise a strategically clever distribution of the space.
- Establish eye contact with your players after gaining possession of the ball.
- Get control of the ball when building up the attack (short passes).
- Only dribble the ball in a 1:1 situation right in front of the opponents' goal.
- Back pass when the intended pass position is marked.

Organisation

Play 5:5 in one half of the pitch with four small goals on each half.

Each team tries to keep the ball in its own lines as long as possible in order to score a goal in one of the two goals (see Fig. 43).

Fig. 43

Number of Players:	Ten.
Equipment:	Several balls, five coloured bibs, eight flag poles.
Load:	3 x 10 minutes with short breaks (active ball exercises e.g. 4:1).

Variation:
- Goal assignment diagonally.
- Increase of playing time (reduction of the number of series).
- Limit ball contact in each team's own half of the pitch to two per player.
- Goals only count if preceded by a wall pass.
- Goals scored by heading count double.
- Form three teams. Two teams play each other, the other rests by doing exercises with the ball.

Note

The coach should encourage the players to perform tricks, feints and dribble the ball again and again in order to improve individual technique.

☒ Professionals

☒ Amateurs

☒ Juniors

☐ Children/Teenagers

Objectives

The through pass as a way of a quick attack, soccer-related endurance, individual techniques.

Didactic and methodical hints

- Do not let break off eye contact with the player in the "zone".
- A through pass is only practical when the opposing team has moved up and can be overrun by the fast strikers.
- Play a through pass when the other team is not properly positioned on the pitch.
- A through pass can be used as a way of freeing up play.
- A through pass can be used to start a counter by the other team, to force a shift in the centre of play, to get play going on the wings or to bridge the midfield.

Organisation

The players play in teams of 3:3 and 1:1 in a marked section of the pitch. The team with the ball makes a through pass when the player in the marked "zone" can shake off his marker (see Fig. 44). After the player has gained control of the ball, the game continues with a new ball in the square.

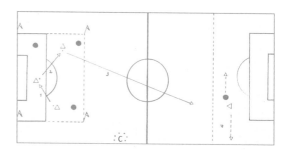

Fig. 44

Number of Players:	Eight.
Equipment:	Many balls, four flag poles, two marking cones and four coloured bibs.
Load:	5 x 7 minutes.
Variation:	– Increase of the section so that the players have to run longer distances and have more space to play.
	– Increase of the number of players (4:4; 5:5), thus putting them under more pressure.
	– Limit ball contact between the players to two per player.
	– Only two pairs of players are in the "zone".
	– Play on two small goals in the marked section of the pitch.
	– A shot at goal after the through pass.
	– Increase playing time, thereby reducing the number of series.
	– Form three teams. Two play each other and the third rests and carries out active ball exercises.

Note

This game requires increased attention and good peripheral vision on the part of the player making the pass. For this reason this exercise should be carried out at the beginning of a training session to take advantage of the players' mental and physical freshness.

The through pass can also be improved by individual training in strike techniques and posture etc.

⊠ Professionals

⊠ Amateurs

⊠ Juniors

☐ Children/Teenagers

Objectives

Playing shot at goal, creative playing, individual techniques, anaerobic endurance.

Didactic and methodical hints

– Demand for covering ground, dribble and wall passes.

– Look for tackling an opponent.

– Force rapid diversion and tricks.

– Demand for skilled ball control after a tackle.

– Demand for a surprising shot at goal, or for outplaying the goalkeeper.

– Get the players to shake off their opponents and get into space.

Organisation

Plays 2:2 with two "neutral" players on a large goal.

Two pairs of players play in a marked square, and, through skilled team work, including the "neutrals", they try to score a goal as quickly as possible.

If a goal is scored, or if the ball gets out, the game starts again at the centre line (see Fig. 45).

Fig. 45

Number of Players:	Six players and one goalkeeper.
Equipment:	Many balls, two red and two green bibs, four flag poles.
Load:	5 x 2 minutes per pair.
Variation:	– Increase of the number of players (this decreases the space on the pitch).
	– Form several teams which play on a rotation basis.
	– The "neutrals" are only allowed to pass the ball directly to another player.
	– Increase of the number of series (while shortening playing time per series).
	– After every round the "neutrals" change places with other players.

Note

After such a unit do not get the players to do speed exercises. Rather they should carry out recovery training.

This form of game can only be carried out with children and teenagers if passing skills have been perfected.

☐ Professionals
☒ Amateurs
☒ Juniors
☐ Children/Teenagers

Objectives

"Shooting" – improving shooting, tackling, creativity with the ball and soccer-related endurance.

Didactic and methodical hints

- Get the players into skilled teamwork.
- Maintain eye contact with your team-mates.
- After having safe control of the ball dribble or pass it immediately.
- Pass to a player outside of the marked out square.
- Practise and force new tricks and feints.
- A shot at goal should be done in a "cool" manner.

Organisation

The players play 3:3 in a marked out square in front of the penalty area.
Both teams try to score a goal as quickly as possible in teamwork with the players posted outside the square (see Fig. 46).

Fig. 46

Number of Players: Nine.

Equipment: Several balls, four coloured bibs, four flag poles.

Load: 10 x 2 minutes with short breaks.

Variation:
- Reduction of the number of players (while reducing the number of series).
- The two players acting as pass points around the playing pitch change after a given time. Two tired players go to the pass points.
- Limited ball contact to two contacts per player.

Note

The coach should always get the players to attempt a shot at goal resolutely (as though under competitive conditions).

☒ Professionals
☒ Amateurs
☒ Juniors
☐ Children/Teenagers

Objectives

Majority, anaerobic endurance.

Didactic and methodical hints

- Get the players to spread themselves out properly on the pitch.
- Demand for a quick pass and for getting into space.
- Force frequent changes of position when a team is on the attack.
- Get a team to concentrate most of its players in the opposing team's defence area when attacking.

Organisation

Get the players to play 5:7 in one half of the pitch using small goals. The larger team tries to score a goal by passing the ball directly.
The smaller team is allowed to kick the ball into the space. (This is part of increasing ball contact – see Fig. 47).

Fig. 47

Number of Players: Twelve.

Equipment: One ball, seven coloured bibs, four flag poles.

Load: 3 x 15 minutes with short breaks and stretching.

Variation: – Extension of the playing time (reduction of series).
- Reduction of the number of players (while shortening playing time).
- The larger team has to pass the ball directly in its own half of the pitch, but in the opponents' half each player may have ball contact twice only.
- Goals can be scored from the front or from behind.
- A goal may only be scored after a wall pass.
- Goals scored by the smaller team count double.

Note

This form of training involves a lot of running. For this reason players should change position more often so that tired players can recover.

☒Professionals

☒ Amateurs

☒ Juniors

☐ Children/Teenagers

Objectives

Minority, anaerobic endurance, marking the space.

Didactic and methodical hints

– Proper distribution of players on the pitch.

– Establish eye contact with each other.

– Also communicate verbally with each other.

– The team moves to the side the ball is on.

– Saving of the ball and start of setting free dribbles (single-footed effort).

– Look for a quick shot at goal.

– Skilfully shielding of the ball from the opponents.

Organisation

The team plays 4:6 in one half of the pitch using small goals. Once it has possession of the ball the smaller team tries to safe it for as long as possible (see Fig.48).

Fig. 48

Number of Players: Ten.

Equipment: One ball, six coloured bibs, four flag poles.

Load: 3 x 15 minutes with short breaks and stretching exercises.

Variation: – Form three teams of four players and keep changing them.
                        – The team in majority may only have two ball contacts per player.
                        – Increase of playing time (reduction of the numbers of series).
                        – Reduction of the playing pitch (makes things easier for the team in minority).

Note

This form of exercise involves a lot of running for the smaller team and should not culminate in speed training.

☒Professionals

☒ Amateurs

☒ Juniors

☐ Children/Teenagers

Objectives

"Pushing" the team to the side of the pitch the ball is on, soccer-related endurance.

Didactic and methodical hints

- Establish eye contact with each other.
- Watch the player with the ball.
- Use of combined player and space marking should be made.
- "Pushing" should not alter the zones each team is in.
- A crossing player is not marked man-to-man, but only the one being next.
- If the team doing the "pushing" is larger, the player with the ball is attacked by two players.

Organisation

Play 6:4 in one half of the pitch with a goalkeeper and with two small goals on the centre line.

The larger team is positioned across the width and depth of the pitch in lines, and has to "push" towards the player with the ball and try to protect both goals (see Fig.49).

Fig. 49

Number of Players:	Ten players and a goal keeper.
Equipment:	Several balls, six coloured bibs and four flag poles.
Load:	3 x 15 minutes with short breaks and stretching exercises.
Variation:	– The larger team is only to have two ball contacts per player. – When building up the smaller team involves the goalkeeper as an additional player on the pitch. – Goals scored by the smaller team count double. – Extension of the playing time (reduction of the number of series). – Form three teams of four players, two of which play each other while the third rests. All three teams take turns continually.

Note
Cool down after the end of training.

☒ Professionals

☒ Amateurs

☒ Juniors

☒ Children/Teenagers

Objectives

Training of free kicks – indirect free kicks, individual techniques.

Didactic and methodical hints

The team on the attack:

– The kicking players should be picked out in advance.

– The free kick should be performed quickly.

– The other players wait for the rebounding ball as well as they secure the rear sections of the pitch.

The team in defence:

– At least five players form a wall.

– The player on the outside stands in line with the near goal post.

– The players forming the wall should not take their arms.

– The players in the wall should jump up and down in order to impede the aiming of the kicking player.

– The goal keeper must be able to see the kicking player.

– If the ball bounces off the wall, the players in the wall should run out towards it immediately.

Organisation

Play 6:5 + one goal keeper on one half of the pitch, using one large and two small goals that stand on the centre line.

Both teams keep playing until the coach whistles for an "indirect" free kick.

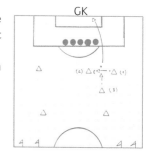

Fig. 50

98

Player (1) passes the ball to player (2), who stops it with the sole of his boot, while player (3) runs up and takes a shot at goal around the wall (see Fig. 50).

Number of Players: Eleven players and one goal keeper.

Equipment: All available balls, six coloured bibs and four goalposts.

Load: 3 x 15 minutes with at least 20 free kicks.

Variation: – As before, except that player (4) stations himself to the left of the wall. player (3) then passes the ball to him (see Fig. 51).

Fig. 51

Note

The players can also practise free kicks as a seperate training. With children and teenagers, free kicks should be practised under easier training conditions.

☒Professionals

☒ Amateurs

☒ Juniors

☒ Children/Teenagers

Objectives

"Corner kicks" as a means of scoring a goal.

Didactic and methodical hints

The team on the attack:

– The kicking player should be picked out in advance.
– Twister away from the goal.
– Twister towards the goal.
– Corner kick towards the near post.
– Corner kick towards the far post.
– Corner kick into the penalty area.
– Corner kick beyond the penalty area.
– Put the player who is best at heading into the penalty area.
– Get the players to carry out a corner kick by a short pass to a nearby team-mate.

The team on the defence:

– The goalkeeper must have a free sight and space for movement.
– The goalkeeper must decide whether he catches the ball or punches it (on bad ground or poor visibilty conditions, and with bodily contact of the opponent, it is better to punch the ball).
– One player covers the near post and another covers the far one.
– The other players mark man-to-man (best players at heading are the last line).
– When the team gains possession of the ball immediate moving out of the penalty area and offering to get the pass.

Organisation

The team plays 6:6 +1 goalkeeper in one half of the pitch using one large and two small goals. Both teams keep playing until the coach awards a corner kick. If the team in defence gains possession of the ball, it has to attack the two small goals at the centre line (see Fig.52).

Fig. 52

Number of Players: Twelve players and one goalkeeper.

Equipment: All available balls, six coloured bibs and four flag poles.

Load: 2 x 20 minutes, with at least 20 corner kicks, and short breaks.

Variation:
– Corner kicks with twist towards the near or the far goalpost.
– Carry out short pass corner kicks to a player standing nearby.
– Corner kicks to outside of the penalty area.
– Extension of playing time.
– Increase of the number of players (11:11).

Note

Corner kick training can also be done as a separate exercise.

When coaching children and teenagers, the exercises should be easier.

☐ Professionals
☒ Amateurs
☒ Juniors
☒ Children/Teenagers

Objectives

"Continuous kicking", soccer–related endurance, creativity in playing, individual techniques, improvisation.

Didactic and methodical hints

– Achieving practiced individual skills with the ball.
– Developing creative ball handling (new tricks and feints).
– Get the players to develop effective teamwork and aggressive tackling.
– Aim at a change of rhythm after gaining possession of the ball.
– Get the players to get into space and to offer themselves for getting a pass.
– Achieve soccer-related endurance.

Organisation

Three teams play 6:6:6 in one half of the pitch using two large goals with a goalkeeper in each of them.

Two teams play each other while the third team has a rest outside the playing area.

After five minutes playing one team goes off the pitch and the third one continues the game and so on.

The score stays the same when the new team takes over (see Fig.53).

Fig. 53

Number of Players:	Eighteen players and two goalkeepers.
Equipment:	All available balls, six red, six green and six yellow bibs.
Load:	2 x 15 minutes.
Variation:	– Extension of playing time.
	– Increase of the number of players.
	– Increase of the size of the playing pitch.
	– Limited ball contact.
	– The team having a rest does technique training recovering.

Note

This form of training is particularly suitable for teenagers as it satisfies their play instinct. The winning team receives a prize as a form of motivation.

For professionals this form of training can be performed as recovery training after a hard weekend game (the players can kick any way they like).

⊠ Professionals

⊠ Amateurs

⊠ Juniors

⊠ Children/Teenagers

Objectives

"Soccer tennis" – individual techniques, teamwork, creativity, finesse.

Didactic and methodical hints

- Demand cooperation between team members.
- Put players of varying abilities in the same team, so that the strong ones can help the weak ones.
- Motivation increases when a tournament is announced.
- Give the weaker players as much ball contacts as they like.
- Demand clever playing.

Organisation

The players play 3:3 on a marked-off 15 x 15 m section of the pitch.
A net is hung through the centre of the pitch at a height of 1.5 m (see Fig. 54).
The ball may be touched with all parts of the body except the hands. If the ball bounces on the ground two consecutive times, this is worth a point.
The ball may only be passed three times within a team's own half. The third pass must be played over the net.
Balls that go under the net count as a fault.
Balls played outside the boundaries of the playing area still count as long as they are passed back over the net or to a player
of the same team (see Fig.54).

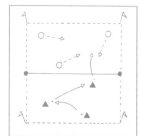

Fig. 54

Number of Players:	Six.
Equipment:	One ball, two goalposts, four flagpoles, a red-white tape or a net.
Load:	2 x 15 minutes with changes of position.
Variation:	– Unlimited ball passes per team.
	– Points scored with the head count double.
	– Form several teams so that they can play each other in turn.
	– Make the players kick the ball only with their "weaker" foot.
	– Extension of playing time.
	– Arrange the teams according to their common features e.g. the smokers, bachelors, married members etc.

Note

This form of practice is a particularly suitable way to start a training session, as well as to finish it provided no other strenuous exercises have taken place before.

For professionals this form of exercise can act as a form of relaxation after a hard game.

☒ Professionals
☒ Amateurs
☒ Juniors
☒ Children/Teenagers

Objectives

Dribble: as speed dribble, creativity, improvisation, anaerobic endurance.

Didactic and methodical hints

- Ensure stopping and controlling the ball.
- Get players to shield the ball by adopting the proper position to it and an opponent.
- Playing without looking at the ball all the time.
- Gaining space after gaining posession of the ball.
- Practising deceptions, tricks and feints.
- Developing confidence when tackling an opponent.
- Looking for opportunities to score a goal.

Organisation

The players play 1:1 using small goals. Each player tries to score a goal as quickly as possible.

The playing field is divided into four pitches of equal size (see Fig.55).

Fig. 55

Number of Players:	Twelve.
Equipment:	Six balls, 24 marker cones, six red bibs.
Load:	1 x 2 minutes with short breaks.
Variation:	– Let the players play into an undefended goal.
	– Shortening of playing time.
	– Increase the number of players (2:2; 3:3; 4:4).
	– Get the players to play without the use of a goal (the ball must be dribbled over the side line).
	– The players are only allowed to dribble with their "weaker" foot.
	– Change of partners.

Note

This form of exercise should be carried out at the start of a training session, as there is a considerable strain on the players' anaerobic endurance, requiring a lot of breaks.

For children and teenagers a playing session should last a maximum of one minute.

☒ Professionals
☒ Amateurs
☒ Juniors
☐ Children/Teenagers

Objectives

"Passing the ball to the striker", accurate passing, soccer-related endurance, short passes.

Didactic and methodical hints

– Require precise passing.
– The "striker" must retain eye contact with his team mates.
– Get the striker to stop and control the ball and run with it properly.
– Goal shot immediately after stopping the ball and getting it under control.

Organisation

Two teams of three players each play in a marked off section of the pitch to the right and left of the centre line. In front of the penalty area there is a marked zone in which the "strikers" are supposed to move.
Immediately after gaining possession of the ball each team tries to pass it to the striker.
The striker must then try to score a goal with a powerful shot.
If he scores a goal his team gets the ball back again (see Fig.56).

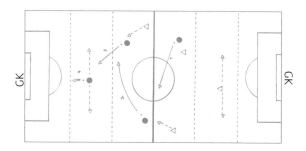

Fig. 56

108

Number of Players:	Eight players and two goalkeepers.
Equipment:	Several balls, eight marker cones, four coloured bibs.
Load:	3 x 15 minutes with short breaks and stretching exercises.
Variation:	– Extension of playing time (reduction of series).
	– Increase of the number of players, thereby increasing the pressure on all the players.
	– The other team marks the "striker" by pressing.
	– By the third ball contact at the latest the ball must be passed to the striker.
	– Each player has to act as striker.
	– If the goalkeeper catches the ball he can throw it impartially into the marked-off section of the pitch.
	– The coach gives the signal for the kick-off.

Note

It is a good idea to let the striker remain in this position for an extended period so that the passing and goal scoring moves with the ball become a habit.

20 The Warm-up

Given the many daily stresses and strains during training, competition and travelling, there is often not enough time for players to recover or gather their strength for the next game. Body and spirit thus run into a physical and psychological deficit which intensifies and often leads to long-lasting injuries and fitness crises.

For this reason it is especially important to make time for recovery and preparation for training and competitions.

A proper warm-up gradually gets the body going, the muscles, cardiovascular system and mind are able to adjust gently to the coming training loads. The gradually rising core body temperature plays an important role here.

As the body warms up the blood circulates better through the muscles, metabolism speeds up and reflexes are quicker.

It also increases the ability to tense and relax the muscles and accelerates the removal of lactates.

The regulation of the body's temperature, which is linked to its warming up, protects the organism from overheating. This renders the body tissues less able to resist heat and also causes the body to sweat in good time, thereby carrying away any surplus heat.

Emotional stability and the right mental state before a competition are an important prerequisite for success in sport. Warming up creates an excellent basis here as well. A "warm-up" reduces so-called "starting nerves"; perception and concentration also increase.

Susceptibility to injury and lack of muscular coordination can be effectively avoided through careful warming up in conjunction with stretching.

The most effective warm-up period before training or a game is about 10-15 minutes. The players should then do stretching exercises for about 5-7 minutes; this is about enough.

Note:
During "warm-ups"; clothing should be appropriate to the sport and to the temperature.

Basic Rules for Warm-ups and Stretching

- Relaxed running, hopping and walking alternately.
- Slow, continuous stretching.
- Twenty seconds of slow pre-stretching and post-stretching (passive stretching).
- For active stretching the player should stretch the muscles for 10 s, relax for 5 s and then stretch for 10 s again.
- The player should not make any bouncy or rocking movements as this may pull or harden the muscles.
- The player should breathe calmly, not jerkily, when performing stretch exercises.

While conducting stretch exercises with the players the coach should proceed according to the muscle groups of the body shown in Fig. 57.

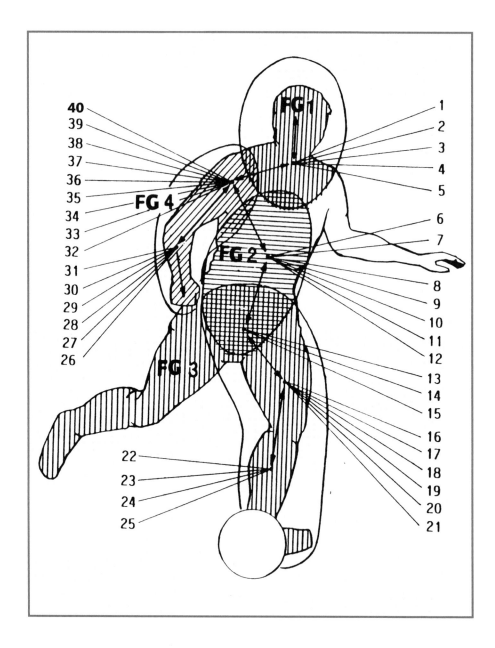

Fig. 57: The four functional groups of muscles according to Knebel

(Source: FRANK,G.: Fußball-Konditionsgymnastik, Frankfurt, M./Berlin 1994)

1 Head turner
   (m. sternocleidomastoideus)
2 Hood muscle
   (m. trapezius)
3 Shoulder blade lifter
   (m. levator)
4 Head of the longest back muscle
   (m. longissimus capitis)
5 Lower neck (vertebrae) muscles
6 Straight stomach muscle
   (m. rectus abdominis)
7 Oblique stomach muscle
   (m. oblique abdominai)
8 Horizontal stomach muscle
   (m. transversus abdominis)
9 Longest back muscle
   (m. longissimus dorsi)
10 Back extensor (m. erector spinae)
11 Muscles of the lower spinal
   column / lower back muscles
12 Serated muscle (m. serratus
   anterior)
13 Back extensor (m. sacrospinalis)
14 Trunk flexor (m. iliopsoas)
15 Gluteal muscle (gluteus maximus)
16 Thigh contractor
   (m. tensor fasciae latae)
17 Tailor muscle (m. sartorius)
18 Leg adductors (m. adductors)
19 Leg abductors (m. abductors)
20 Four-headed knee-joint extensor
   (m. quadriceps)
21 Knee flexor - hamstrings
   (mm. ischiocrurales)
22 Toe extensor
   (m. extensor digitorum longus)

23 Toe flexor
   (m. flexor digitorum longus)
24 Upper ankle muscles
   (dorsal-/plantarflexors)
25 Lower ankle muscles
   (pronators/supinators)
26 Superficial finger flexor
   (m. flexor digitorum superficialis)
27 Deep finger flexor
   (m. flexor digitorum profundus)
28 Finger extensor
   (m. extensor digitorum communis)
29 Thumb muscles (extensors, flexors,
   adductors and adductors)
30 Wrist flexor and extensor
   (m. flexor and extensor carpi radialis
   resp. and ulnaris)
31 Upper arm muscle
   (m. brachioradialis)
32 Double headed elbow extensor
   (m. biceps brachii)
33 Triple headed elbow flexor
   (m. triceps brachii)
34 Inner arm muscle (m. brachialis)
35 Medial and radial rotators
   (pronators and supinators)
36 Chest muscles
   (m. pectoralis major and minor)
37 Delta muscle (m. deltoideus)
38 Broadest back muscle
   (m. latissimus dorsi)
39 Shoulder muscles
   (m. teres major and minor)
40 Supra and infraspinatus
   (m. supra and infra spinatus)

Neck bones and backbones as far as the fifth vertebra.

Exercise 1

Fig. 58

Supine position, the player's knees bent, hands behind the neck. He slowly pulls his body up towards his knees. (This is better known as "sit-ups").

Exercise 2

Fig. 59

Standing position, feet shoulder-width apart. Putting both hands behind his back the player grips his right wrist with his left hand and pulls the wrist diagonally downwards. At the same time he bends his head slowly to the left.

Backbones from the 5th to the 12th backbone, the loin, pelvis and hips.

Exercise 3
Fig. 60

Sitting position, grasping of both knees with both hands and pulling them to the chest.

Exercise 4
Fig. 61

In supine position with his legs bent up towards his chest the player is putting his hands on his knees. From this position he slowly raises his body up towards the knees.

Lower spine, the hip joints, the universal joint, and ilium joint as well as all the extremities.

Exercise 5
Fig. 62

Kneeling position. The player leans back slowly onto his calves and supports his body by resting his hands on his feet behind his posterior.

Exercise 6
Fig. 63

Starting position as if for a sprint. The player puts the toes of one foot at the same level as the knee of the other (kneeling) leg. He then presses his upper body forwards.

Exercise 7
Fig. 64

Long lunge step, the player goes down onto one leg until the thigh is horizontal with the ground and the other leg stretched out behind him with the calf lying flat on the ground from the knee down. The player then slowly lowers his hips towards the ground.

Exercise 8
Fig. 65

Long lunge step, the player goes down onto one leg as in Exercise 7 (above). He then stretches the other leg out sideways from his body until the knee and calf are lying flat on the ground.

Exercise 9
Fig. 66

Long lunge step, the player goes down on one leg as above, bends the other behind him until he can take the ankle in his hand and slowly goes down onto his hips, drawing his ankle to the centre of his posterior.

Exercise 10
Fig. 67

The player sits on the ground, brings the soles of his feet into contact with oneanother and – with each hand on each foot – slowly leans forward.

Exercise 11
Fig. 68

The player stands at a goal post, stretches one leg out behind him with the foot resting flat on the ground and the other leg bent towards the front. He slowly brings his hips forward while keeping the foot of the leg at the rear flat on the ground.

Exercise 12
Fig. 69

Sit-stretches: the player sits on the ground with one leg stretched out in front of him, the other tucked as far as possible into the inner thigh of the stretched leg. From this position he slowly leans his torso forward.

Exercise 13
Fig. 70

The player lies in supine and bends his legs so that the soles of both feet touch each other. He then slowly draws his heels in towards his posterior.

Exercise 14

Fig. 71

The player lies in supine, grasps one knee with both hands and pulls it upwards in the direction of the opposite shoulder.

Exercise 15

Fig. 72

The player assumes a crouching position with his feet flat on the ground and splayed at an angle of about 15°. The knees should be splayed wider than the width of the shoulders and the heels about 10 to 30 cm apart.

Exercise 16

Fig. 73

The player puts one foot flat on the ground, leans forward slightly and puts the other on a raised flat surface such as a bench with the knee bent. He then brings his hips towards the bench, keeping his torso straight.

119

Exercise 17
Fig. 74

The players lies in supine with one arm at 90° to his body and one leg lying at a right angle across the other. With the other arm the player slowly pushes the bent leg down towards the other foot.

Exercise 18
Fig. 75

The player crouches down, places both hands flat on the ground and stretches one leg out sideways from his body.

Exercise 19
Fig. 76

The player stands on the ground, raises one leg behind his body, grasps it with his hand and pulls it slowly towards his other thigh.

Exercise 20

Fig. 77

The player stands on the edge of a step with his legs shoulder-width apart and his heels over the edge of the step. His hands are held firmly by a partner. The player now slowly lowers his heels over the edge of the step.

Exercise 21

Fig. 78

The player lies on his back, grasps the back of one knee with both hands and draws the leg up towards his head.

Shoulder joint, shoulder blade and collar bone along with all of the upper half of the torso.

Exercise 22
Fig. 79

The player stands side-on to the goal post or similar with legs shoulder-width apart. He stretches out his arm, grasps the post, turns his head slowly towards his other shoulder and looks to the rear.

Exercise 23
Fig. 80

The player stands and clasps his hands, arms outstretched, above his head, turns the palms outwards and stretches his arms (with the palms still clasped) horizontally out in front of his body at head height.

Exercise 24

Fig. 81

The player stands with his feet apart (shoulder-width), clasps his hands with the palms outwards and raises them up over his head, stretching them at the same time.

Exercise 25

Fig. 82

The player stands with his feet shoulder-width apart. With one hand he reaches behind his head for the opposite shoulder, the other hand grips the other elbow and slowly presses the arm downwards.

(Source: FRANK, G.: Trainingsprogramme Fußball, Meyer & Meyer, Aachen 1997)

21 The Cool-down

"Cooling down" is nothing more than an active relaxation phase after a strenuous match or intensive training.
The function of the cooling down period is to slowly bring the body down from the level of competition load to normal .
The breathing rate decreases, heart rate and muscle tone are reduced, energy use sinks and psychological tension decreases markedly.

The enormous competition and training loads with up to two training units a day actually promote a systematic "anti-tiring".

In cooling down a distinction is made between active and passive regeneration. Here, "slowly running around" or "slowly walking around" play an important role. 10 to 15 minutes of this activity is reasonable. If the surface of the pitch permits, having the players run barefoot is a good idea.

A warm bath, a long shower, or short sessions in the sauna may be used as passive anti-tiring measures. These may be followed by light massages.

If the above measures are not possible, a gentle stretching programme in the changing room is recommended.

22 Index*

Press marking	1
Pressing	20
Quick reacting	8
Running behind the defence	12
Saving the ball	5
Short-distance passing	40
Soccer-related endurance	1/6/8/11/12/14/18/19/20/21/ 23/26/27/28/29/31/34/37/40
Soccer tennis	38
Speed endurance	13
Sprint speed	12/13/17/22
Sweeper behind the defence	16
Sweeper in front of the defence	15
Tackling	1/31
Teamwork	25/38
Through passes	14/29
Understanding the game	28
Wall passes	7
Warming up in the form of a game	24
Wing playing	18
Zone marking	2/21/23/34

* Note: The index refers to the individual training units.

23 Bibliography

Anderson, B.: Stretching. Waldeck-Dehringshausen 1996

Bisanz, G./Gerich, G.: Fußball - Training, Technik, Taktik. Reinbek bei Hamburg 1995.

Frank, G.: Fußball - Konditionsgymnastik. Frankfurt/Main 1994

Frank, G.: Trainingsprogramme Fußball. Aachen 1997

Mayer, R.: Fußball trainieren. Reinbek bei Hamburg 1996

Müller-Wohlfahrt, H.-W./Montag, H.-J.: Verletzt ... was tun? Pfaffenweiler 1996

Rutemöller, E.: Die Spielsysteme bei der WM - in: Fußballtraining number 6. 1996 Philippka-Verlag Münster.

Weineck, J.: Optimales Fußballtraining. Erlangen 1992.

Wienecke, E.: Laktatdiagnostik out? - in: Fußballtraining number 4. 1997. Philippka -Verlag Münster.

Periodicals:

Fußballtraining, (publisher) G. Bisanz, Philippka-Verlag, Münster